The Ultimate Guide To:

Communication Skills!

Improve Self Confidence, Leadership, And Charisma To Persuade And Influence People!

I0486038

Ryan Cooper

STOP!!! Before you read any further....Would you like to know the Secrets of Transforming your life, overcome insecurities, develop leadership skills, and undeniable confidence in your personal, professional, and relationship life?

If your answer is yes, then you are not alone. Thousands of people are looking for the secret to have unstoppable confidence and self-driven power in all areas of their lives.

If you have been searching for these answers without much luck, you're in the right place!

Not only will you gain incredible insight in this book, but because I want to make sure to give you as much value as possible, right now for a limited time you can get full **100% FREE access to a VIP bonus EBook** entitled **LIMITLESS ENERGY!**

Legal Notice

Disclaimer Notice

Table Of Contents

Introduction

I want to thank you and congratulate you for purchasing the book, *"Communication Skills: The Ultimate Guide To Communication Skills! - Improve Self Confidence, Leadership, And Charisma To Persuade And Influence People!"*.

This "Communication Skills" book contains proven steps and strategies on how to become a more effective communicator, leader, and listener!

In writing this book I decided I wanted to help people to not only become fantastic communicators and great leaders, but I also think it is equally important to become more self confident and to gain skills to persuade and influence people!

In this book's seven simple chapters, you will learn a lot about practical communication skills that you have to master in order to be the best communicator that you can be.

Thanks again for purchasing this book, I hope you enjoy it!

Chapter 1 - Body Language And Communication Skills

Have you ever found yourself in a situation wherein you do not believe what another person is saying to you? Have you ever found yourself not believing that the person speaking to you has enough credibility to say what he is saying? Perhaps, you have found nodding physically but deep inside, your mind is shouting "No!"

The big difference between what a person says and the way we get their message is determined by the speaker's body language marked by the non-verbal cues and signals that they are using. Once you become more aware of these signals, cues, and signs, you will have an edge when it comes to understanding other people and developing your own communication skills.

Sometimes, we encounter situations wherein the subtle and the not-so-subtle signals affect our overall understanding of a message that has been conveyed. These signals usually consist of facial expressions, body movements, gestures, and the shirts in the body posture. The way a person sits, talks, and walks tell a lot about their message because these are reflections of what's going on inside their heads.

In order to become a better communicator yourself, you need to have a better understanding of the body language. This will help you become more aware with the way you choose to communicate. At the same time, you will learn to read what's on other people's minds. To increase your understanding of what other people are truly saying, you also need to become aware of the signals you are personally sending through your own body language.

Note that there are common signs and signals that you have to be aware of. These usually determine whether the person or the message (or both) are worth believing. The following are some of the things that you have to look out for whenever you communicate (note that the "communicator" can be yourself or other people):

> *) The communicator's posture: A credible person usually stands tall. His shoulders are always leaning towards the

back to avoid curved impression.

*) The communicator's eye contact: This tells a lot about the communicator's sincerity. A communicator who has a good intent usually is confident of looking in the other party's eye. Eye contact usually greatly complements a smiling face.

*) The communicator's gestures with his arms and hands: A good and credible communicator moves his arms and hands in a purposeful and deliberate manner.

*) The communicator's speech: A good communicator never leaves anything to doubt. Usually, a confident communicator delivers his speech clearly and slowly.

*) Tone of the voice: A good communicator keeps the tone of his voice as low as possible. The lower the tone, the more confident and more serious he seems.

Aside from decoding other peoples' body language and signals, an understanding of these elements are truly useful in effectively communicating what you have to say to other people. The knowledge of body language will help you send emotions, feelings, and intent that you want your audience to see. This way, you can create a better impression.

For instance, when you are about to enter a communication situation, of course you want to appear that you are a person of sufficient authority on the subject matter. Of course, you also want to show everyone how confident you are of what you are about to say. By controlling your gestures, posture, tone of voice, among others, you can send all the "confidence signals" despite the fact that deep inside, butterflies are flying in your stomach.

Body language has a great impact in the way you deal with others and in the manner you choose to communicate. They are taken to reflect what's happening deep inside your mind, body, and emotion.

Aside from those mentioned earlier, body language includes leg movements, muscle tension, skin coloring (for example, becoming white faced or flushed red), perspiration rate, and the rate of breathing.

These signals may also vary across cultures. Different nations have different kinds of norms and traditions that have to be carefully accounted for. When you try to get to know a person, these should be included in what you are asking and verifying.

Chapter 2- Basic Communication Skills You Need To Know

The capability to communicate with other people is considered to be one of life's most important skills.

It is a necessity to define what communication exactly is. For our purposes, communication can be defined as the act of taking an effort to transfer a certain piece of information from one location to another using your voice (vocal), and digital or printed media (written) such as emails, magazines, websites, and books. In other instances, the communication can be visual (e.g. maps, graphs, charts, and logos) or non-verbal (gestures, body movements and body language, as well as pitch or tone of the voice). Now that these are clear, we can proceed with the discussion.

Communication skills can be gauged by looking at how well a person is able to transmit a message or information to his intended receiver. Once a person effectively develops his communication skills, he will expect a better life because he will have an idea on how to deal with other people in different social settings – career-related, parties, and family events among others. For instance, if you have great communication skills, you would know what is expected of you even before you take on the stage. That way, you will know how to convey messages in a clear and accurate manner – the way you originally intended it to be. If at this point, you are not that confident of your skills connected to communication, do not fret! It is not yet too late to develop it. In this chapter, you will be given a walk through to the basic communication skills that you need to know.

Communication Skill that you Need to Know #1: Interpersonal Communication Skills

Strictly defined, interpersonal skills refer to the communication skills that are used in dealing with other people face-to-face. What we are saying here is that it is of utmost importance to send our message to our intended audience, but our speaking skills and verbal communication skills can only take us too far. There is more into communication. Our gestures, non-verbal signals, body language, expressions on our face, and even our appearance tells a lot about what we are saying. Therefore, interpersonal communication skills factor in personal presentation, non-verbal communication, and personal appearance.

Truth be told, when we say interpersonal communication, it consist of forty-five percent listening. However, most people take the listening part for granted. Listening should be active and by doing so, you will be able avoid misunderstandings. Most people listen inattentively and that has a very deep impact in your interpersonal communication. With proper listening, you get to clarify and reflect more effectively leading to a more sincere and empathic conversation.

When you have above par skills in interpersonal communication, you have greater potential in working with teams and groups. You can move with ease and confidence in formal and informal settings and situations. These can ultimately lead to highly desirable and strong relationship and connections with other people, which are both essential in having a better kind of understanding and communication.

Interpersonal communication skills are important in the process of developing other key skills in life. The capability to communicate well with the people around you is the most common premise needed in bringing solutions to many problems that are encountered both in your career or family life. On the other hand, this is also instrumental in making important decisions in other areas. With great interpersonal communication, you will be able to communicate highly complicated information in a simple manner. That way, you can deliver appropriate decisions with the necessary assistance from key players.

Communication Skill that you Need to Know #2: Presentation Skills

For many people, presentation skills may be used not as frequently as other skills presented in this chapter; however, no one will know when you'll need it especially in the workplace. There are different times in your life wherein you will need to present particular information to groups of people – be it in informal and formal settings.

Imagining yourself doing a presentation in front of any audience may sound a bit difficult especially for beginners, but one can gain confidence doing it as time goes by and with frequent practice. With frequent practice and finding opportunities to plan, you will soon find yourself losing the fear over doing public presentations.

Communication Skill that you Need to Know #3: Written Communication Schools

Direct interaction is just one way of communicating with other people. In other instances, especially when dealing with hierarchy, you have to know how to communicate yourself effectively without a single spoken word.

The capability to communicate in writing through a channel should be honed. This is one of the key communication skills that you have to perfect because it is not a thing exclusive for professional journalists or authors. If your communication skill in writing is poor, your readers might get frustrated because they won't get what you are really saying. In other instances, poor written communication skills might even hurt your credibility; it can even bring great damage to you and your profession.

Note that you might need to look into your skills and knowledge in grammar, spelling, sentence structure, and informal and formal writing styles. By doing so, you will be able to communicate all your ideas seamlessly. You will also have a deeper understanding of what sort of messages you send to other people through writing.

Communication Skill that you Need to Know #4: Personal Communication Skills

Personal communication skills are often taken for granted by many, but these are the skills that we use in order to keep a healthy mind and body. By developing this skill, you can be sure that your other communication skills will improve. This involves building up your self-esteem and improving your self-confidence.

Of course, you have to look at your personal presentation and your physical appearance. Admit it, the way you look and the way you carry yourself has a great bearing to how you are perceived by the people around you. Therefore, it affects all your communication processes.

In the process of getting a deeper understanding of what is happening within you, you will have a more optimistic and a better relaxed outlook in your life. That way, you are likely to take on a more charismatic personality. Charisma is a trait that will be further discussed in a latter chapter in this compendium.

Additionally, you will have better communication skills if you have acceptable personal communication skills. This will enable you to become more assertive. Assertiveness is a desirable trait because it helps you get a fair share of things.

During stressful times, you get to communicate is a less effective manner. This happens especially when you get too angry. By studying how to be more effective with your personal communication skills, you will know how to reduce, control, and manage all the sources of your stress.

Chapter 3- Key Strategies For Self Confidence And Communication

The manner by which we communicate with the people around us, most especially when we confront the most intense situations, has an effect to our level of self-confidence. More often than not, ineffective communication serves as a catalyst to poor relationship with other people.

Many people fall into the trap of getting too eager to get their message and point across. Once you are too much into "winning" arguments and over-enthusiastically pushing your point, you might end up being an ineffective communicator. Sad but true. By being too "pushy," you end up not being heard – by choice. This results to the feeling of exhaustion, the lack of mutual respect, and the impression of not being appreciated.

In this chapter, you will learn the value of having a perfect mix of communication and confidence. Once you gain the proper amount of confidence, you can expect that you are able to express yourself and your feelings more effectively. Also, you will have the capability to say what you truly need. Lastly and most importantly, you will be able to build mutual trust with the people around you. With that, you will feel that everything you say is properly heard.

Important Characteristics of a Confident Communicator

(1) <u>An effective and confident communicator knows how to use his body language</u>. Under this, you need to learn how to effectively look others in their eyes, call other people by their names, and paint a smile on your face. Additionally, a confident person has a good body posture and a stance that is open. Their faces usually give a non-threatening impression. Also, an effective and confident communicator finds it easy to talk with any person around him.

(2) <u>An effective and confident communicator, by all means, avoids sarcasm and other snide remarks</u>. This is true during times of peace. This is equally true during times of war. When a confident communicator is bashed by the other party, he keeps his composure. He avoids finding himself in a position wherein he will

appear defensive and insecure. Note that sarcasm is a signal that you are losing your patience and that you can no longer tolerate other people. This should not be the case if you are truly confident about yourself. You know what you are made of no matter what other people say.

(3) <u>An effective and confident communicator knows how to effectively keep his cool</u>. Usually, they do not reach a point where the situation is heated. But during rare instances when they are caught in such tense situations, they are wise enough to stick to what's true. They try their best to express their emotions through their carefully picked words rather than their behavior. They avoid increasing the volume of their voices, too. Other unnecessary actions like slamming the door, uttering threats, and outburst of emotions are generally avoided. A good communicator's goal is to make the other party understand his point without getting carried away with their emotions.

(4) <u>An effective and confident communicator makes sure that he listens and validates points encountered</u>. A good communicator knows that it is a two-way road. He is generous in giving time and attention to the other party – with the highest hopes that he will be given the chance to speak up afterwards. He acts with utmost respect. In addition, he knows how to do validation. When a person validates, note that he does not really have to agree with what has been said. Rather, validation is a genuine attempt to come up with an acceptable level of understanding of what has been uttered by the other party.

(5) <u>An effective and confident communicator knows how to chill out or relax</u>. To avoid frustration, forget the usual "I am on the right side" point of view. Relax, you do not have to be right at all times. It is important to be mindful of the situation at the moment. Avoid setting emotional expectations to avoid frustration and disappointment. Be open to the possibility that things might not go as you expect – but at least, do your part.

(6) <u>An effective and confident communicator is mindful of what other people are saying and doing</u>. For example, if you know that the person you wish to talk with is busy doing his favorite thing from 3pm to 4pm, then you should be mindful enough about these details as a signal of respect. Additionally, never ever waste the time of other people.

(7) <u>An effective and confident communicator, when communicating verbally, uses "and" instead of "but" more often</u>. For any situation they face, they consciously avoid "but" by all means. In speaking situations, "but" sounds like a sign of hesitation. Sometimes, it even feels like your putting your guards up. If you do not wish to send confusing signals to your audience, avoid "but" because it might even sound like a back-handed complement or a snide remark in disguise.

(8) <u>An effective and confident communicator, tries to be fair with his speaking partner</u>. Note that he tries his best not to dominate the conversation. They allow other people to speak their minds out. Moreover, they sincerely put an effort to hear them out.

(9) <u>An effective and confident communicator knows that it is beyond "all or nothing</u>." Things cannot be simplified by saying "always" or "never." In fact, having these kinds of qualifiers in mind can even complicate things. There is such a thing as a grey area, and that's where intelligent people are. To be more effective, make sure that your observations are subjective and not lying on extreme ends.

Note that for highly complex situations, an effective and confident communicator is always aware of what's going on within him. He watches all the thoughts that run in his mind, and he has the capability to regulate. An effective communicator knows when to speak out and when exactly to listen. Finally, a good and effective communicator shows respect to the people with whom he is interacting with.

Chapter 4- Using Charisma To Influence And Persuade Any Audience

Commonly, people struggle with coming up with the exact definition of charisma. What's more challenging for them is how to fuse the concept of charisma with day-to-day communication situations.

At the ultimate, "charisma" is just an end result of fusing together the best practices presented in the previous chapters in this compendium. It is a product of continuous pursuit for communication excellence and well-honed interpersonal skills. Note that people are not born with these skills; it is up to the person to develop them.

Steps to become truly charismatic

To become truly charismatic, a person needs to give attention to the way he interacts with others. It is a process of highlighting all the positive traits and making a good impression on other people. A person is truly charismatic if he uses his skills to influence other people and convince them to take his side. This is true in various facets of life – ideological, professional, and social aspects can be considered here. For these particular reasons, charisma is often taken to be an important ingredient of leadership. Without charisma, it is impossible for anyone to become a great and successful leader.

Usually, when you say "charismatic," you usually think of a person who is seen positively by the public. These people are usually very successfully and influential, but this does not mean that only public figures can have charisma. Within your circle, you can display your charisma.

Being charismatic takes confidence

Confidence has been a recurring buzzword in this compendium, but this is the necessary trait if you truly want to be an effective communicator. If you are confident in carrying yourself and in conveying your intended message despite the variety of situations that you may face, and if you do not struggle in facing different kinds of audience, then you have a great potential as a charismatic communicator. A person who is blessed with charisma has an "outer glow" causing other people around them to be empowered by their mere presence. That way, the communication as a process is greatly enhanced. People with charisma are people who are confident without getting egotistic or boastful.

Being charismatic requires optimism

Along with charisma and confidence, a great communicator knows how to appear positive and hopeful despite the odds. It means that they are putting conscious efforts to look at the bright side – be it on situations, people, or events. As a result, the outward manifestation is bubbliness and cheerfulness. People with charisma have the innate capability to give strong and lasting encouragement to others. As a result, people they touch become more enthusiastic in things that they do. To be truly optimistic, one has to think positively so that negotiations handled in the future will be successful. According to experts, optimism also plays a big role in problem solving.

Being charismatic necessitates emotional strength

A person is capable of displaying various degrees of emotional strength. They use their emotions to their advantage without losing their sense of truthfulness and their sincerity. Also, they try their best to be serene and calm at all times despite the struggle within.

Being charismatic requires being interested and being interesting

Just like respect, interest has to be reciprocated. A charismatic person knows that in order to be looked at with utmost interest, he should also appear interested at what other people are saying. Charismatic communicators make it a point to keep their stories interesting – on the other hand, they find it easy to find what's interesting in any story presented to them.

Being interesting involves practicing conciseness and clarity. They also know when to take on a serious tone and when to inject humor in things that they say. That way, they are able to maintain, their audience's focus. Charismatic people become more interesting because of their mastery of small group, large group, and one-to-one communication situations. They also take on a relaxed, open, and appropriate body language. As much as possible, they maintain their eye contact because it communicates sincerity and interest. In short, effort to be inclusive is exerted at all times.

People who are charismatic know how to reciprocate the interest given to them by their intended audience. In order to do so, they ask questions to clarify, and they express their opinions and reactions to what other people are saying. People who are charismatic know exactly how to get the most heartfelt and most honest responses with the people they communicate with. People who are charismatic know how to show empathy and consideration to other people. The details of previous conversations are also recalled to display trust, confidence, and respect.

Being charismatic calls for occasional display of intelligence

To gain credibility and to enhance integrity, a person has to know how to begin interesting conversations. That's one thing, but it is equally important to know how to maintain conversations. And yes, that requires a high level of intelligence to do that.

By being intelligent, the intention is not to show off. Rather, intelligence should be properly used. For example, to keep conversations interesting, a person needs to be updated with general knowledge and with current events. With the proper use of intelligence, awkward situations and dead air will be avoided.

Being charismatic requires attention to the little details

If you want to master the art of charisma, paying attention to the smallest of details serve as the capstone. This way, you know the little things that occur at the level of interpersonal communication. The result is a more dynamic, passionate, and enthusiastic process of exchanging messages and information. Therefore, being charismatic would involve more than giving an influential front; it is actually a result of having a deeper understanding of the dynamic yet beautiful process of communication.

Chapter 5- Using Listening Skills To Be A More Effective Communicator

To be a truly effective communicator, you need to master the art of listening. It is one of the most important skills that you can hone and improve further. The manner by which you listen has a great effect on how effective you are in conveying message and it is a clear determinant of your job effectiveness. Also, it tells a lot about the quality of our relationship with the people around us.

We listen in order to understand, to enjoy, to learn, and to acquire specific information. In almost everything we do, we use our listening faculty. According to studies, we better remember things we hear than those we acquire through other means. Therefore, if we decide to improve our listening skill, we will definitely improve and benefit from it.

Active Listening – What is it?

Active listening is the process by which we exert effort to consciously hear a person out – not just what the person says, but what exactly he is trying to communicate. That way, we get a better grasp of the information.

In order to enhance a person's active listening skills, you have to let your conversation partner know that you are truly listening to what he has to say. This is important because it shows respect and it unleashes sincerity and truth in the communication process. Again, validation and affirmation does not only have to happen verbally; most of the time, it can be done using non-verbal cues and other elements of the body language.

To become a true active listener, you have to bear in mind the following key elements:

*) **Give your full attention**: This can be shown by giving your undivided attention. If possible, drop everything else; just give your 100 percent to the conversation going on. Look at the speaker directly. Put away all potential sources of distraction. Clear your mind of preparation for rebuttal. And finally, you have to pay attention to the body language as well.

*)**Show that you are truly listening:** You need to complement

attention with your gesture and body language. To let the speaker know that you are truly listening, try to nod from time to time. Use your facial expressions to show your reactions. Also, it is essential to keep an inviting and open posture. Lastly, occasional non-verbal encouragements will help you show your sincere intent to listen.

*) **Give feedback to the speaker:** Personal judgments, beliefs, opinions, assumptions, and filters can make messages appear different once we receive them. To avoid confusion, as much as possible, try to ask questions and clarify important points so that you will gain a deep understanding of what's being said. Of course, you might need to reflect on what was said. By providing feedback, the speaker will know what things to define further and which points to give more attention to.

*) **Avoid coming up with hasty judgment:** If possible, let the speaker finish first. Do not interrupt for the sake of airing non-concurrent or opposing views. This might lead to frustration on the part of the speaker, and your level of understanding will suffer if you air counter arguments and rebuttals right away.

*) **Try to respond in an appropriate manner:** An active listener is seen as a role model for advocating for understanding and respect. He aims to gain perspective and understanding. Additionally, he knows that attacking the speaker does not achieve anything good.

Begin utilizing the art and science of active listening now and you will feel the "magic" that it can do to your effectiveness as a communicator. In the long run, you will be delighted with increased productivity in the workplace and higher quality of relationships with people around you.

Chapter 6- Key Strategies For Leadership And Communication

By equipping communicators the skills necessary to lead and communicate, they are likely to enjoy a wide array of benefits. For example, the alignment of goals, efforts, and results, are likely to improve. In addition, if ever decisions are made, it will effortlessly gain the support of the majority which will make the implementation less problematic. Resistance will go down and submission is to the authority of the leader/communicator is likely to increase. Subordinates are likely to appreciate their jobs more and they see their contribution to the overall success of the organization.

A good communicator knows that he has to hone his leadership skills, even if he is not yet in the position of power. Everyone has the capability and potential to lead, so no one can tell when this can be tapped, so the following skills have to be developed:

*) Creation of a robust strategy for communicating with others

*) Respect and understanding of difference in culture and its effect to appropriate communication strategies

*) Capability to communicate insights, and not mere bits of information, to aid in the propagation of rationale and context

*) Skill to tell a story that is relatable and memorable

*) Conciseness coupled with sensitivity

*) The talent to anticipate the reaction after delivering any kind of message

*) Applying communication skills to tell a story of change, to communicate undesirable news, and to make connections

Communicators should be aware of the fact that they should bear leadership skills in order to become better in conveying their message. This way, they will know how to create other leaders who are capable of communicating significant changes in the organization. Additionally, they need to be prepared in merging with other organizations and communicate effectively despite the odds that the change may bring. Lastly, effective communicators can create or even change an organization's culture so that it will be more responsive to the changes.

Chapter 7 - Social Skills And Everyday Strategies For Relationship Communication

To build great relationships with other people, one has to have the basic social skills. This will greatly improve one's communication skills. In turn, this helps a lot in reducing anxiety and stress brought about by relating with other people.

Avoiding social situations won't help. Without exposing yourself to social situations, you will never have the chance to build up your self-esteem and self-confidence through healthy interactions with other people. Additionally, choosing to stay in solitude will not help in developing your communication skills. These two aspects of communication can only be honed by creating meaningful relationships with other people.

Skills on conversation

To lessen social anxiety, one has to hone his skills in conversing with others. This might seem a bit of a struggle at first, but with constant practice, you will realize that it becomes a more pleasant and more desirable activity through time.

In developing your conversation skills, you have to assess yourself first. Ask yourself if you are having trouble in beginning a conversation. Additionally, do you find it more difficult to maintain a conversation because you are running out of topics to talk about? Do you find it difficult to take your turn in speaking?

Importance of being assertive

A key to more meaningful relationship is by being more assertive. This way, you can be expressive of your needs, feelings, and your wants without sacrificing the respect of other person. Whenever you use assertion, you get to express what you want without being judgmental or threatening.

Many fall into the trap of falling into the extremes – some are too aggressive while others are too passive. By exhibiting the perfect balance, you will learn the art of assertiveness. Note that assertiveness is not a skill that you can learn because you already have it within you. All you have to do is try to use it more often and be more comfortable with your assertion.

Conclusion

Thank you again for purchasing this book on Communication Skills!

I am extremely excited to pass this information along to you, and I am so happy that you now have read and can hopefully implement these strategies going forward.

I hope this book was able to help you understand all the aspects of excellent communication and how to use them to your advantage.

The next step is to get started using this information and begin living a much more fulfilling life!

Please don't be someone who just reads this information and doesn't apply it, the strategies in this book will only benefit you if you use them!

If you know of anyone else that could benefit from the information presented here please inform them of this book.

Finally, if you enjoyed this book and feel it has added value to your life in any way, please take the time to share your thoughts and post a review on Amazon. It'd be greatly appreciated!

Thank you and good luck!

Preview Of:

The Ultimate Guide To:

<u>Self Confidence!</u>

Stop Shyness And Self Doubt, Develop Great Social Skills, Build Charisma, And Begin Feeling Good About Yourself!

Introduction

I want to thank you and congratulate you for purchasing the book, *"Self Confidence: The Ultimate Guide To Self Confidence! - Stop Shyness And Self Doubt, Develop Great Social Skills, Build Charisma, And Begin Feeling Good About Yourself"*

This "Self Confidence" book contains proven steps and strategies on how to Stop Shyness and Self Doubt for good!

This ultimate guide to self confidence is an easy to implement guide with proven steps and strategies to build self confidence and charisma and to begin feeling good about yourself!

It is aimed to help you overcome your social anxieties; free yourself from the bondage of self-doubt; and unleash the confidence in you. Confidence is what fuels the person to move forward. It is the driving force that enables us to overcome any inhibitions that may hinder our progress.

Confident people are attractive. They are usually more successful in life than those who prefer to work in the sidelines. If you are confident, you can be who you want to be and you can achieve whatever your goals are. It will be possible with the help of this book.

Success is just around the corner. If you are confident, you will be able to chase your dreams without second guessing yourself, and start actually living your dreams instead of sitting on the sidelines. Be free. Be socially skilled...Be popular...

Be confident and go to greater heights...

Thanks again for purchasing this book, I hope you enjoy it!

Chapter 1: Self-Confidence And Its Importance

Imagine a room full of people and suddenly a confident person walks in, what do you think will happen? If that person were to speak, do you think everyone would listen? Does a confident person give up easily when assigned with a difficult task? Does he run into a corner at the first sight of failure?

Confident people get the attention of everyone when they enter a room full of people. When they speak, everyone listens. When they are assigned with a difficult task, they don't give up easily and instead they are grateful to be given the opportunity to showcase their talents. When they think they are about to fail, confident people moves forward and say "Bring it on or I can do this!"

Self-confidence is a trait that everyone wants to have but only a few will be able to get.

So, how do we define self-confidence? When you know what you are capable of, you take pride in your own value as a person, and when you are able to convey that to others, that is self-confidence. Arrogance is not self-confidence for it is when you have an unrealistic view of yourself; you think you are better than you actually are. In contrast, when you think that you are less valuable than others, you have a low self-esteem.

So why is self-confidence important?

Before we enumerate the importance of self-confidence, it is imperative for us to define our goals first. You have to know what you are aiming for. Otherwise, developing self-confidence will only lead you nowhere than where you have started.

Here are some of the reasons why self-confidence is important:

1. **Confidence is an effective ingredient in relationships**: There are lots of researchers who believe that confidence is more important than good looks when it comes to relationships. Men and women find confidence as an attractive trait to the opposite sex. A confident woman walks in and men start tailing her. Similarly, a confident

smile to a woman can capture her attention. Confidence is not only important in the dating phase of the relationship. Couples who are both confident in themselves and in the relationship are more likely to last than those who are overshadowed by their partner.

2. **Confidence leads to career growth**: Confident people naturally do well in everything. Even when they fail, they think that they at least know what they need to do to succeed next time. This type of mentality often attracts growth and promotion at work. When you believe in your abilities as a sales person, and when you believe in the product you sell, there is a greater chance that you surpass the required quota for sales and that definitely is an accomplishment. Studies have also shown that people who started developing confidence earlier in life are more likely to succeed than those who were only taught to aim for higher standards.

3. **Confidence gains people's trust**: Confidence breeds trust. People who are confident about their skills and talents are trusted by their colleagues to finish the job, and do it well. They are trusted by their classmates to win a contest on behalf of their class. Confident people are trusted by the people around them to excel in any field they choose to take. Although it may be a little burdensome, the trust that people give can somehow make a confident person strive harder and achieve what he is intended to accomplish; actually making him more confident in the process.

4. **Confidence defines how we live our life**: If you are a person who always want to be alone and work in the sidelines, and if you don't feel good about yourself because you believe you're not good enough, you are most probably living a miserable life. If you are confident with whom you are, people will be drawn to you regardless of your outward appearance. When you enjoy being with people, you get to enjoy life and everything it offers.

5. **Confidence helps us to communicate better and get what we want in life**: If you are confident, you are not afraid to say what you want. You are capable of saying

no when you need to, and people will always value your opinions. Learning to say what you want can make a big impact in your life. Express yourself honestly and appropriately will definitely get you what you want in life.

Thanks for Previewing My Exciting Book Entitled:

"Self Confidence: Stop Shyness And Self Doubt, Develop Great Social Skills, Build Charisma, And Begin Feeling Good About Yourself!"

To purchase this book, simply go to the Amazon Kindle store and simply search:

"SELF CONFIDENCE"

Then just scroll down until you see my book. You will know it is mine because you will see my name "Ryan Cooper" underneath the title.

Alternatively, you can visit my author page on Amazon to see this book and other work I have done. Thanks so much, and please don't forget your free bonuses

DON'T LEAVE YET! - CHECK OUT YOUR FREE BONUSES BELOW!

Free Bonus Offer: Get Free Access To The <u>PotentialRise.com</u> VIP Newsletter!

Once you enter your email address you will immediately get free access to this awesome newsletter!

But wait, right now if you join now for free you will also get free access to the "LIMITLESS ENERGY" free EBook!

To claim both your FREE VIP NEWSLETTER MEMBERSHIP and your FREE BONUS Ebook on LIMITLESS ENERGY!

<u>Just Go To:</u>

www.PotentialRise.com